Bible Studies
for the Lovers of God

A STUDY OF PHILIPPIANS

BY
BOB & ROSE WEINER

*"that I may know Him and the power of His resurrection
and the fellowship of His sufferings . . ."*

Phil. 3:10

MARANATHA PUBLICATIONS, INC.
P.O. BOX 1799
Gainesville, FL 32602

Cover Photograph
by Jerry Sieve

Bible Studies
For the Lovers of God

Table of Contents

Scripture references in *Bible Studies for the Lovers of God* are designed for use with the *New American Standard Version* unless otherwise noted.

BIBLE STUDIES
FOR THE LOVERS OF GOD

A STUDY OF PHILIPPIANS

INTRODUCTION

The Epistle to the Philippians, one of Paul's prison epistles, was written from Rome. The theme of this epistle is, "The Joy of Christian Grace and Experience". Paul himself demonstrated the greatest joy in the greatest suffering and humiliation. The key verse is, "For to me to live is Christ, and to die is gain". (Phil. 1:21)

Paul was Nero's prisoner, yet the epistle fairly shouts with triumph, the words "joy" and "rejoice" appearing frequently. We find in this epistle that true Christian experience is the outworking, whatever our circumstances may be, of the life, nature, and mind of Christ. The contents of this epistle cover four basic areas of Christian experience:

1. *It is Full of Christ*—Our relationship to Christ, our possession in Christ, our responsibility to Christ, are all wonderfully set forth.

2. *It is Full of Joy*—"Rejoice in the Lord" is the burden of the apostle's message. The word "joy" or "rejoice" is found 16 times here. The life of praise under all circumstances is clearly set forth. Prison walls could not restrain the apostle's song of rejoicing in his ever-present Lord.

3. *It is Full of Holy-Mindedness*—The Greek word for mind, "phronein," (which speaks of a mind intently directed in a practical way in the good interest of someone) occurs ten times. The apostle would have the Christians at Philippi set their heart and mind and will in holy concentration of of attention upon one thing, the glory of their God and Savior. He longed to see the mind of Christ fully reproduced in them. If their mind was right, their life would be found right also.

4. *It is Full of Fellowship*—The Greek preposition "sun" is used which denotes the closest fellowship and communion of interest, the most intimate association. As we study this epistle we feel how close and real are the bonds which bind together all who love our Lord Jesus Christ.

(Philippians 1:1-7)

1. What word of comfort and promise is given to us in the opening of Paul's letter to the Philippians? (Phil. 1:6)

   _____

2. We see the deep fellowship and communion that Paul and the believers have as they are bound together in Christ. What statements does Paul make that reveal his deep love for them? (Phil. 1:3-8)
   a. (v.3) _____
   b. (v.4) _____
   c. (v.5) _____
   d. (v.7) _____
   e. (v.7) _____
   f. (v.8) _____

1

STUDY 1

THE ALL-SUFFICIENCY
OF CHRIST

I. CHRIST, THE CHRISTIAN'S LIFE: REJOICING IN SPITE OF SUFFERING (Phil. 1:8-30)

1. What is Paul's prayer for us? (Phil. 1:9-11)
   a. (v.9) _____
   b. (v.10) _____
   c. (v.10) _____
   d. (v.11) _____

2. Paul's prayer for believers to be filled with the love of God, which operates according to knowledge and discernment, and to be filled with the fruits of righteousness is a prayer from the very heart of God. We see a prophetic fulfillment of this prayer in Isaiah 11:1-5.
   a. Who is the shoot spoken of in Isa. 11:1?

   _____

   b. Who is the branch? (Isa. 11:1) Compare with John 15:5.

   _____

3. How does Isaiah describe the "Spirit of the Lord" which will be resting upon the Branch, (the Church)? (Isa. 11:2)
   a. _____
   b. _____
   c. _____

   While this passage is traditionally recognized as a messianic prophesy which Jesus fulfilled, it can also be extended to apply to His Church. Jesus in His suffering brought many sons to glory; (Hebrews 2:10-11). It was His desire that the glory and the Spirit upon Him also rest on His Church; (John 14:16,17, John 17:22). In John 15:5, Jesus identifies the Branches as His disciples, thus extending the Messianic anointing to all His followers.

4. When this Spirit rests upon the believers, what will happen? (Isa. 11:3-5)
   a. (v.3) _____
   b. (v.3) _____
   c. (v.3) _____
   d. (v.4) _____
   e. (v.4) _____
   f. (v.4) _____
   g. (v.4) _____
   h. (v.5) _____
   i. (v.5) _____

5. Although Paul is in prison and in chains for preaching the gospel, what is his attitude? (Phil. 1:18) _____

6. What does he rejoice in? (Phil. 1:12-18)
   a. (v.12) _____
   b. (v.13) _____
   c. (v.14) _____
   d. (v.18) _____

7. If any of us were in prison, the desire of our heart might be to get out as soon as possible. Yet what is the desire of Paul's heart, his hope, his expectation? (Phil. 1:20-21)

   a. (v.20) _____

   b. (v.20) _____

   c. (v.21) _____

8. When Paul leaves his earthly body where will he go? (Phil. 1:23)

   _____

   Where are the Christians who have died? (II Cor. 5:8)

   _____

9. Although Paul had an earnest longing to depart from this life to be with Christ, he knew in his spirit that his time was not yet. Why? (Phil. 1:24-26)

   _____

10. Paul exhorts the believers to continue in conversation or conduct that becomes the gospel of Christ. What conduct was that? (Phil. 1:27-28)

    a. (v.27) _____

    b. (v.27) _____

    c. (v.27) _____

    d. (v.28) _____

11. As the believers stand fearlessly against man, proclaiming the gospel, what two things is it evidence of? (Phil. 1:28)

    a. _____

    b. _____

12. What did Paul mean by this being a sign of destruction for them? (II Thes. 1:6)

    _____

13. What did Jesus Himself say in regards to this ? (Heb. 10:30)

    _____

14. Therefore, according to the law of Moses, what does the Lord exhort us to do? (Lev. 19:18)

    _____
    _____

15. Again, in this same passage from Philippians, Paul says that as believers stand fearlessly against man proclaiming the gospel, it is an evidence of salvation for you. What does he mean by this? (II Thes. 1:4-5, 11)

    _____
    _____

16. Actually, what does this persecution do for us spiritually? (II Cor. 4:17; Rom. 8:18)

    _____

17. As we suffer with Him, what will happen? (Rom. 8:17)

    _____

18. What are we not to be surprised by? (I Pet. 4:12)

    _____

19. What is the purpose of this "fiery ordeal" and what should be our response? (I Pet. 4:12-13)

    a. _____

    b. _____

20. If you are reviled for the name of Christ, what is it a sign of ? (I Pet. 4:14)

    _____

21. If anyone suffers as a Christian, what should he do? (I Pet. 4:16)

    _____

22. Where must judgment begin? (I Pet. 4:17)

    _____

23. What is difficult? (I Pet. 4:18)

_____

This salvation spoken of here is not eternal life, for eternal life is in the Son and is given to all those who believe in the Lord Jesus. This salvation is that total sanctification of the spirit, soul, and body, that we may bear His image. God's hand of judgment comes against the righteous in order to burn away anything that will not reflect His glory. The Amplified Version of the Bible speaks of these believers that are judged in such a manner as being the *uncompromisingly righteous*.

24. What is the fruit of the uncompromisingly righteous and what does he do? (Prov. 11:30) [Please give your answer from the Amplified Version quoted below].

"The fruit of the uncompromisingly righteous is a tree of life, and he who is wise captures human lives for God as a fisher of men—he gathers and receives them for eternity."

   a. _____

   b. _____

25. We discovered earlier that Paul spoke about this suffering and persecution coming upon us in order to make us "worthy." Jesus Himself spoke of those who were found worthy. What did Jesus say those who are worthy would attain to? (Luke 20:34-35)

_____

This age He is speaking of is the millennial age, the age of the Kingdom of God when Jesus Himself will rule and reign on the earth for 1,000 years. Again this is not speaking of eternal life.

26. What did Paul himself desire to attain to? (Phil. 3:10-11)

_____

We must note here that the resurrection of the dead does not automatically come with dying and going to heaven. For this we all qualify for through faith in the Son. But this resurrection of the dead was something that the greatest apostle was seeking himself to attain to and qualify for.

27. Paul likens this to running a race. What exhortation does he give? (I Cor. 9:24-27)

   a. (v.24) _____

   b. (v.25) _____

   c. (v.26) _____

   d. (v.27) _____

28. What was Paul's desire? (I Cor. 9:27)

_____

29. What two names does Jesus give to those who attain to the resurrection and are found worthy? (Luke 20:36)

   a. _____

   b. _____

30. What quality of life do those who have a part in the first resurrection display? (Rev. 20:6)

_____

31. What did those who have a part in the first resurrection do in the face of persecution? (Rev. 20:4) _____

We see that those who were worthy stood fearlessly in the face of persecution even to the laying down of their lives for the testimony of Jesus. They also did not yield to the beast, the worldly system. To be a part of the first resurrection does not necessarily mean that you have to be a martyr, but you must be *willing* to lay down your life even unto death.

5

32. Therefore, what should we do if we suffer according to the will of God? (I Peter 4:19)
   a. _____
   b. _____

33. What privilege is given to all believers who will boldly proclaim Christ? (Phil. 1:29)
   _____

II. CHRIST, THE CHRISTIAN'S PATTERN: REJOICING IN LOWLY SERVICE
   (Phil. 2:1-30)

   1. What attitude of Christian behavior does Paul exhort the believers to walk in? (Phil. 2:1-4)
      a. (v.2) _____
      b. (v.2) _____
      c. (v.2) _____
      d. (v.2) _____
      e. (v.3) _____
      f. (v.3) _____
      _____
      g. (v.4) _____
      _____

   2. What does Paul liken the above attitude of mind and action to? (Phil. 2:5)
      _____

   3. Let us look at Christ's example. What was Christ's mind or attitude? (Phil. 2:6-8)
      a. (v.6) _____
      b. (v.7) _____
      c. (v.7) _____
      d. (v.7) _____
      e. (v.8) _____
      f. (v.8) _____

   4. Christ emptied Himself of the glory that was His, He laid down all of His power and became
      a man. By what power did Christ operate while on earth? (Acts 10:38)
      _____

   5. Shortly after Jesus was baptized with the Holy Ghost, He performed the miracle of turning
      water into wine. Did He do any miracles before this? (John 2:11) _____

   6. As a result of Christ's humbling Himself, what happened? (Phil. 2:9)
      a. _____
      b. _____

   7. Peter also exhorts us to be humble. What are we to do? (I Peter 5:5-6)
      a. (v.5) _____
      b. (v.5) _____
      c. (v.6) _____

   8. If we humble ourselves, what will God do? (I Peter 5:6)
      _____

   9. What power and authority is in the name of Christ? (Phil. 2:10-11)
      a. _____
      b. _____

10. What three inhabited worlds are pointed out by this scripture? (Phil. 2:10)

    a. _____

    b. _____

    c. _____

Paul exhorts us in Phil. 2:12 to work out our own salvation with fear and trembling. This is not a statement telling us to work our way to heaven, because no man is justified by works in the sight of God. Only by faith in Jesus Christ is the man justified. This is a statement for Christians to be sober and watchful and diligent. Let us look at a few verses concerning this.

11. What has God appointed us to? (I Thes. 5:9)

    _____

12. What is this the salvation of? (I Thes. 5:23)

    a. _____

    b. _____

    c. _____

13. Who will perform this sanctification? (I Thes. 5:24; II Thes. 2:13)

    a. (5:24) _____

    b. (2:13) _____

14. How can we purify our souls? (I Peter 1:22)

    _____

15. Read II Timothy 2:16-22. In order to be a vessel of God fit for the Master's use, what are we to do?

    a. (v.16) _____

    b. (v.19) _____

    c. (v.22) _____

    d. (v.22) _____

16. What exhortation do we have from Peter regarding the obtaining of this total salvation? (II Peter 1:10)

    _____

17. If we do the things that Peter lists in chapter 1, he says we shall never fall. What are these things? (II Peter 1:3-9)

    a. (v.3) _____

    b. (v.4) _____

    c. (v.5) _____

    d. (v.5) _____

    e. (v.5) _____

    f. (v.6) _____

    g. (v.6) _____

    h. (v.6) _____

    i. (v.7) _____

    j. (v.7) _____

18. As we follow in this diligent path seeking the Kingdom of God first, what will happen? (II Peter 1:11) _____

    _____

This entrance into His Kingdom is more than salvation; but it is reigning in this life and being an example of His Kingdom on earth as it is in heaven.

19. In order for us to obtain this glorious salvation of body, soul and spirit, we must set our minds toward heavenly things. How does Paul tell us this will take place? (Phil. 2:13)

_____

20. If we do all things without grumbling and disputing, what will we be and do? (Phil. 2:14-16)
    a. (v.15) _____
    b. (v.15) _____
    c. (v.15) _____
    d. (v.15) _____
    e. (v.16) _____
    f. (v.16) _____

God Desires To Possess The Soul of Man. It Is The Prize of God.

All that is of the soul life, the *I think,* the *I want,* and the *I feel* must come under the sanctifying work of the Spirit of God by obedience to the truth.

As Jesus taught, "He who loves his soul life—*I think, I want,* and *I feel*—shall lose it, and he who hates his soul life—hates the *I think,* the *I want,* and the *I feel*—in this world, shall keep his soul life to life eternal."

21. For what two things does Jesus say we ought to lay down the *I think,* the *I want,* and the *I feel*? (Mark 8:35)
    a. _____
    b. _____
22. What made God say that David was a man after His own heart? (Acts 13:22)

_____

23. What did Jesus say about His own actions and why? (John 5:30)
    a. _____
    b. _____

A beautiful picture of this subduing of the soul life is given in parable form in the story of Gideon's army. Read Judges 7:16-20.

24. What was inside the pitchers? (Judges 7:16)

_____

The Spirit of the believer is like a torch hidden in a pitcher or earthen vessel. It burns but is covered by the unbroken soul life of man.

25. What happened when the pitchers were smashed? (Judges 7:19-20)

_____

_____

So as the *I think,* the *I want,* and the *I feel* are smashed, as were the pitchers of Gideon's army, we will truly appear as lights of the world, holding forth the word of life, which is the sword of the Lord, in the midst of a crooked and perverse generation.

—NOTES—

STUDY 2

THE TRUE SERVANTS
OF GOD

I. THE FELLOWSHIP AND LOVE OF THE SAINTS

1. What did Paul say about himself and his life? (Phil. 2:17)

_____

The Living Bible says it this way: "And if my lifeblood is, so to speak, to be poured out over your faith which I am offering up to God as a sacrifice—even then I will be glad, and will share my joy with each of you. For you should be happy about this too, and rejoice with me for having this privilege of dying for you."

2. What did Jesus say was the greatest sign of love? (John 15:13)

_____

3. In the Song of Solomon we find some beautiful verses that tell of the love of Christ for His Bride. What is the depth of love described here? (Song 8:6-7)
   a. (v.6) _____
   b. (v.7) _____
   c. (v.7) _____
   d. (v.7) _____

This is the love Jesus has shown to us and we are exhorted to love one another as He has loved us. This is the commitment and love that God longs for us to have one for another. As we grow and are knit together as a body committed one to another, this deep devotion and love will grow in us.

4. How is the growth of the body described in Ephesians 4:16?

_____

_____

_____

5. As we come to know the love of God, laying down our life for our brother, what will happen? (Eph. 3:19)

_____

6. When we are filled up with the fullness of God, what will be seen in the church? (I John 4:8)

_____

7. We have said earlier that the book of Philippians is full of fellowship. What bonds of fellowship were there between Paul, Timothy, Epaphroditus, and the church at Philippi? (Phil. 2: 19-30)
   a. (v.19) _____
   b. (v.20) _____
   c. (v.22) _____
   d. (v.25) _____
   e. (v.25) _____
   f. (v.25) _____
   g. (v.26) _____
   h. (v.26) _____
   i. (v.27) _____
   j. (v.28) _____
   k. (v.30) _____

This is a beautiful example of the deep bonds of love the early Christians had for one another.

8. Why was Epaphroditus sick?   (Phil. 2:30)

   _____

II. WARNING AGAINST FALSE PROPHETS AND TEACHERS

1. What three things did Paul exhort the believers to beware of? (Phil. 3:2)
   a. _____
   b. _____
   c. _____
2. Who are the dogs? (Isa. 56:10-12)
   a. (v.10) _____
   b. (v.10) _____
   c. (v.10) _____
   d. (v.10) _____
   e. (v.11) _____
   f. (v.11) _____
   g. (v.11) _____
   h. (v.12) _____
   i. (v.12) _____

This is the picture of the leaders and false prophets of the harlot system of whom in Revelation it is written, "She has made the inhabitants of earth *drunk* with the wine of her fornication". These leaders are blind, not being able to discern the time, being ignorant of God's Word. Each one is trying to build his own kingdom, crying peace when there is no peace. These are smooth mouthed prophets that lull and ease people to sleep in their sins, not calling for repentance from dead works and faith toward God. These are the false prophets of the latter day.

3. Why can't these leaders discern the times which are at hand and hear what the Spirit is saying to the churches? (Jer. 6:10)

   _____

4. What else does God have against these leaders? (Jer. 6:13-19)
   a. (v.13)_____
   b. (v.13)_____
   c. (v.14)_____
   d. (v.14)_____
   e. (v.15)_____
   f. (v.16)_____
   g. (v.17)_____
   h. (v.19)_____
5. Who are the true circumcision (the true Jews)? (Phil. 3:3; Rom. 2:28-29)
   a. (v.3) _____
   b. (v.3) _____
   c. (v.3) _____
   d. (v.29) _____
   e. (v.29) _____
   f. (v.29) _____
   g. (v.29) _____

6. Who are Abraham's seed? (Rom. 4:11-12)
   a. _____
   b. _____

7. If we are Christ's then whose seed are we and what are our rights? (Ga. 3:29, 14)
   a. (v.29) _____
   b. (v.29) _____
   c. (v.14) _____
   d. (v.14) _____

These scriptures are basic keys for interpreting Old Testament scripture, for whatever applies to the Jews in the natural applies to the children of faith in the spiritual. Paul's warning here, too, was against Judaizing legalists who maintained that simple faith in the finished work of Christ was not sufficient, but had to be supplemented by law works—circumcision, ceremonial feasts, fasts, etc. Paul points out that true circumcision is a spiritual exercise embodying service rendered by the Holy Spirit and evidenced by glorying in Christ alone. The circumcised heart places *no confidence in the self life.*

8. If Paul did base his righteousness and acceptance before God on works, what type of record did he have in the flesh? (Phil. 3:4-7)
   a. (v.5) _____
   b. (v.5) _____
   c. (v.5) _____
   d. (v.5) _____
   e. (v.5) _____
   f. (v.6) _____
   g. (v.6) _____

If anyone could have been justified before God by a good show in the flesh, Paul would have been. From the Hebrew point of view he is seen to be the proud possessor of great wealth and merit derived from the highest code of divine law, the Mosaic law.

9. Paul himself saw no value in all of his fleshly efforts. What is his opinion of them? (Phil. 3:7-8)
   a. (v.7) _____
   b. (v.8) _____
   c. (v.8) _____

10. What does Paul exhort us to do regarding works in the flesh? (Phil. 3:3)

_____

11. What was the desire of Paul's heart concerning righteousness? (Phil. 3:9)
   a. _____
   b. _____
   c. _____

Paul here clearly puts down all claims of acceptance and favor before God on the grounds of personal merit. Paul instead said that this righteousness obtained through the law is but rubbish compared to the spotless righteousness which God has provided in Christ through faith.

12. As we lay hold of the righteousness that is by faith, apart from works, then what will happen to our pride? (I Cor 1:26-29)

_____

13. Therefore, who will receive the glory for our spiritual progress, growth, and development? (I Cor. 1:30-31)

_____

14. What are we to glory in according to Jer. 9:23-24?

_____

—NOTES—

STUDY 3

THE HIGH
CALLING OF GOD

We have now come to the portion of the book of Philippians in which Paul sets forth his goal, his vision, and the driving force behind his Christian walk. "Without a vision, the people perish." Paul had started in the runner's course. He was pressing on to grasp that for which Christ had already laid hold of for him. The only safe and normal attitude for the Christian is one of seeking for nobler attainment and higher achievement—continued progress in spiritual things. There is no such state as inertia here. If there is no progress, there will be backsliding. As we study this portion of Philippians we hope to get a glimpse of this vision and goal that Paul had set before him, which he called "the mark for the prize of the high calling of God in Christ Jesus." As we look into the prize which is set before us we will find that it involves total redemption of the man, body, soul, and spirit. Let us search the scriptures so that we might set before our eyes a burning light so that we can run the race with a definite aim in mind; that we might fight the fight of faith, not just beating the air, but striking death blows to the enemy; and let us run in such a way that we might hit our mark, and obtain the prize. (Taken from I Cor. 9:25-27)

I. THE CRY OF PAUL'S HEART (A CRY OF ALL TRUE LOVERS OF GOD)

   1. What was the cry and consuming passion of Paul's heart? (Phil. 3:10)
      a. _____
      b. _____
      c. _____
      d. _____
   2. What is eternal life? (John 17:3)

      _____

The heart cry of Paul was to know God, to have fellowship with Him, and to share with Him in every aspect of his life. This heart cry of all true lovers of God echoes through the scriptures.

   3. In Song of Solomon, which is an allegory of the love between Christ and His church, we see this same cry repeated. What is the cry that goes forth from the heart? (Song 1:1-4)
      a. (v.2) _____
      b. (v.2) _____
      c. (v.3) _____
      d. (v.4) _____
      e. (v.4) _____
      f. (v.4) _____
      g. (v.4) _____
      h. (v.4) _____
   4. What does the prophet Hosea say of this cry of love? (Hosea 11:4)
      a. _____
      b. _____
      c. _____

This is the cry of the love between Christ and all those who truly love Him. This is the cry of the committed, of those who are willing to sacrifice all to follow Him. As we follow on to know the Lord we find this cry ringing out in our heart.

5. Why did Paul want to share in Christ's sufferings? (Rom. 8:17; II Tim. 2:12; I Pet. 4:13-14)

    a. _____

    b. _____

    c. _____

6. Why did Paul want to be made comformable to Christ's death?   (II Cor. 4:10-11; II Tim. 2:11; Rom. 6:4-5; John 12:24-25)

    a. _____

    b. _____

    c. _____

    d. _____

    e. _____

In Philippians 4:10-11 Paul says he longs to know the power of the resurrection and longs to attain to the resurrection of the dead. Let us read this passage from the Amplified Version for more clarity.

"For my determined purpose is that I may know Him—that I may progressively become more deeply and intimately acquainted with Him, perceiving and recognizing and understanding (the wonders of His person) more strongly and more clearly. And that I may in the same way come to know the power outflowing from His resurrection (which it exerts over believers) and that I may so share His sufferings as to be continually transformed (in spirit into His likeness) to His death (in hope) that if possible I may attain to (the spiritual and moral) resurrection *(that lifts me) out from among the dead even while in the body.*"

Paul is speaking in this passage that the goal and cry of his heart is for total salvation of his spirit, soul, and body.

7. What has God appointed us and called us to? (I Thes. 5:9; II Thes. 2:14)

    a. _____

    b. _____

8. What does this salvation involve? (I Thes. 5:23)

    a. _____

    b. _____

    c. _____

9. Who will bring this salvation to pass in our lives? (I Thes. 5:24)

    _____

We see then that we have been called to total transformation of not only spirit, but also our soul and body.

II. REDEMPTION OF THE SOUL

1. How will this salvation or transformation of the soul be accomplished? (II Cor. 3:18; James 1:21)

    a. _____

    _____

    b. _____

    _____

2. What is the word implanted? (James 1:22)

    _____

This means not only must we hear the Word, but we must do it until it becomes such a part of us that we can't help but live it. If we know God has provided healing, we must act on it. If we know that we can trust Him to guide our paths, we must cease from worry and fret. In general, we must not only know the Word, but we must seek to act it out in our every day life.

3. What is said of one who is totally transformed in his soul? (Ps. 45:13-14)

    a. (v.13) _____

    b. (v.13) _____

    c. (v.14) _____

4. What will the bride of Christ be like in the last days? (Song 6:8-10)

    a. (v.9) _____

    b. (v.9) _____

    c. (v.9) _____

    d. (v.9) _____

    e. (v.10) _____

    f. (v.10) _____

    g. (v.10) _____

    h. (v.10) _____

5. What did Paul say was God's purpose for those whom he has called? (Rom. 8:29)

_____

This was the cry of Paul's heart and his vision and goal, total transformation of his soul into the exact image of Christ. This is what he was pressing into, and striving to apprehend.

6. What will be the outcome of our faith? (I Peter 1:9)

_____

III. REDEMPTION OF THE BODY

1. As we continue to walk in the Spirit, what will happen to our mortal body? (Rom. 8:11)

_____

2. As we walk in the Spirit, what other promises do we have for our body? (Ps. 103:3-5; Isa. 40:28-31)

    a. (v.3) _____

    b. (v.4) _____

    c. (v.5) _____

    d. (v.29) _____

    e. (v.29) _____

    f. (v.31) _____

    g. (v.31) _____

    h. (v.31) _____

3. What are some examples of divine health in the old Testament? (Josh. 14:7-11; Gen. 5:23-27; II Kings 2:9-11)

    a. _____

    b. _____

    c. _____

In Hebrews it says that we are under a better covenant which was established upon better promises than those people under the old covenant.

4. What did Paul say he was groaning for in II Cor. 5:2-5?
   a. (v.2) _____
   b. (v.3) _____
   c. (v.4) _____
   d. (v.4) _____

So we see here that Paul was longing not to be taken in death but to *overcome* death.

5. Where does this idea fit in the purpose of God? (II Cor. 5:5)
   _____

Read Hebrews 2:1-9

6. What has God done for us positionally? (Heb. 2:8)
   _____

7. Yet what is our experience? (Heb. 2:8)
   _____

8. What has Jesus done for us? (Heb. 2:9, 14-15)
   a. _____
   b. _____
   c. _____

9. What else has Jesus done for us? (II Tim. 1:10)
   a. _____
   b. _____

10. What has the law of the Spirit of life in Christ Jesus made us free from? (Rom. 8:2)
    _____

We see then that provision has been made for us through Jesus to overcome even death. All things have been put under our feet, yet Paul says although provision is there, we have not come into the experiencing of it.

11. We know that Paul and the overcomers of the early church died not receiving this promise. Why? (Heb. 11:13, 39-40)
    _____

12. Was God pleased with them? (Heb. 11:39)
    _____

13. Is the Lord slack in fulfilling His promise? (II Pet. 3:8-9)
    _____

According to scripture God has given certain promises and has set certain times for their fulfillment. We see this for example in the promises of the Messiah and the time when He appeared, the promises of the restoration of Israel and the time (1948) when God began to fulfill the promise. There is also a set time when the saints of God shall rise up in the Spirit and overcome in all things. This promise has been given to all the prophets of God down through the ages, and it was given to Paul and the early church. It is what Paul calls "the manifestation of God's sons." But there is a time for its fulfillment set by the Father.

14. What does David say concerning this time? (Ps. 102:13-18)
    a. _____
    b. _____

15. What does Daniel say concerning this time? (Dan. 7:22)
    _____

16. When the time comes, appointed of the Father for the saints to overcome in all things, what will happen? (Dan. 7:18, 26, 27)
    a. (v.18) _____
    b. (v.18) _____
    c. (v.26) _____
    d. (v.26) _____
    e. (v.27) _____
    _____

17. What does Haggai say concerning this day? (Hag. 2:21-23)
    a. (v.21) _____
    b. (v.22) _____
    c. (v.23) _____
18. What does Isaiah say concerning that day? (Isa. 60:19-22)
    a. (v.19) _____
    b. (v.20) _____
    c. (v.21) _____
    d. (v.21) _____
    e. (v.21) _____
    f. (v.22) _____
19. When will this come to pass? (Isa. 60:22)
    _____

20. What does Zechariah say concerning that day? (Zech. 14:20-21)
    _____
    _____

21. What does Malachi say concerning that day? (Mal. 3:17-18; 4:1-3)
    a. (3:17) _____
    b. (3:17) _____
    c. (3:18) _____
    d. (4:1) _____
    e. (4:2) _____
    f. (4:2) _____
    g. (4:3) _____

This is the great day of the overcomers that has been spoken of and foretold by all the prophets. This is the day that Paul was looking for and the goal which he was pressing toward, and the high calling that he was seeking to obtain.

22. What does Paul say that the whole creation is groaning for? (Rom. 8:18-25)
    a. (v.19) _____
    b. (v.21) _____
    _____
    c. (v.23) _____
23. When shall this salvation be revealed? (I Pet. 1:3-5) _____
    _____

24. When will the end come and how long must Christ reign until He returns? (I Cor. 15:24-25)
    a. _____
    b. _____

19

25. What is the last enemy to be destroyed? (I Cor. 15:26)

_____

Christ is the head of His body, the church. The feet speak of that part of His body that is walking upon the earth. Christ Himself has already overcome in all things and has already been seated above all principalities and powers. But His body has not experiencially come into all of Christ's provision for it. However, there will be a generation which will receive total redemption of body, soul, and spirit, and shall overcome in all things. This body of overcomers is being raised up now all over the earth. They are overcoming daily by the power of the Spirit and belief of the truth. Their souls are being transformed from glory to glory into the image of the Lord. When this last enemy, death, is overcome, Jesus shall return and the age of His Kingdom shall be ushered in.

Read I Cor. 15:51-57

26. In light of all these things what does Paul exhort us to do? (Phil. 3:13-15)
    a. _____
    b. _____
    c. _____
    d. _____

—NOTES—

STUDY 4

EXHORTATION TO
HOLY-MINDEDNESS

Having set before the eyes of the Philippian church as a burning light the mark of the High Calling of God in Christ Jesus, Paul throughout the rest of the epistle exhorts the believers to holy-mindedness, unity, joy and prayer. We have stated earlier that the Epistle to the Philippians is 1) full of Christ, 2) full of joy, 3) full of fellowship, and 4) full of holymindedness. The apostle would have the Christians at Philippi set their heart and mind and will in *holy* concentration of attention upon "one thing", the glory of their God and Savior. He longed to see the mind of Christ fully reproduced in them. If their minds were right, their life would be right also.

I. EXHORTATION TO WALK IN THE TRUTH YOU HAVE RECEIVED

1. In light of the High Calling of God which is set before us, what does Paul exhort us to do? (Phil. 3:16)

   _____

There is no state of lukewarmness in this Christian life. If there is no progress, there will be backsliding. Therefore, it is important for us to walk in the light of everything that we have received, being doers of the Word.

2. Paul is exhorting us in the above passage to walk in the light that we have received. What are we to do according to Hebrews 2:1, 3?
   a. _____
   b. _____
3. What does John exhort us to do concerning this? (Rev. 2:25-26)
   a. _____
   b. _____
      _____
4. What does Peter exhort us to do? (II Pet. 3:11-18)
   a. (v.11) _____
   b. (v.12) _____
   c. (v.14) _____
   d. (v.14) _____
   e. (v.14) _____
   f. (v.17) _____

II. EXHORTATION TO WALK IN THE EXAMPLE OF THE GODLY

1. What does Paul say to the believers at Philippi which we also should be able to say unto others? (Phil. 3:17)
   a. _____
   b. _____
2. In what four areas does Paul exhort the believers to follow him? (Phil. 4:9)
   a. _____
   b. _____
   c. _____
   d. _____

3. Paul exhorts young people who are following the Lord to let no man despise them because they are young, but to be an example to the believers. In what areas are young people to be an example and what exhortation does Paul give them? (I Tim. 4:12-14)

a. (v.12) _____ f. (v.13) _____
b. (v.12) _____ g. (v.13) _____
c. (v.12) _____ h. (v.13) _____
d. (v.12) _____ i. (v.14) _____
e. (v.12) _____

4. What example does Paul exhort these people to follow and set before others?
Aged Men (Titus 2:2)

a. _____ d. _____
b. _____ e. _____
c. _____ f. _____

Aged Women and Young Women (Titus 2:3-5)

a. (v.3) _____ g. (v.5) _____
b. (v.3) _____ h. (v.5) _____
c. (v.3) _____ i. (v.5) _____
d. (v.3) _____ j. (v.5) _____
e. (v.4) _____ k. (v.5) _____
f. (v.4) _____

Young Men (Titus 2:6-8)

a. (v.6) _____ d. (v.7) _____
b. (v.7) _____ e. (v.8) _____
c. (v.7) _____

Servants (Employees) (Titus 2:9-10)

a. (v.9) _____ d. (v.10) _____
b. (v.9) _____ e. (v.10) _____
c. (v.9) _____

III. EXHORTATION TO BEWARE OF ENEMIES OF THE CROSS

1. What does Paul call those who do not walk in this manner? (Phil. 3:18)

_____

2. What description is given of these enemies? (Phil. 3:19)

a. _____
b. _____
c. _____
d. _____

3. What does Peter say concerning these enemies of the cross? (II Peter 2:10)

a. _____
b. _____
c. _____
d. _____
e. _____

4. If any man refuses to believe in the doctrine of holiness or godliness and teaches otherwise saying it is impossible to live holy in this present life, what does Paul say about them? (I Tim. 6:3-5)

a. (v.4) _____
b. (v.4) _____

c. (v.4) _____

d. (v.5) _____

e. (v.5) _____

5. What does this false teaching produce? (I Tim. 6:4-5)

a. (v.4) _____ d. (v.4)_____

b. (v.4) _____ e. (v.5)_____

c. (v.4) _____

6. Those who cause division are also enemies of the cross for they go around trying to divide God's people and Jesus said a house divided against itself cannot stand. What are we to do about those who cause division? (Rom. 16:17)

a. _____

b. _____

7. How do they bring deception? (Rom. 16:18)

a. _____

b. _____

IV. EXHORTATION TO SET OUR MIND ON HEAVENLY THINGS

1. Where is our conversation (a more literal translation of conversation would be citizenship or place of residence)? (Phil. 3:20)

_____

2. Where are we seated? (Eph. 2:6)

_____

3. What is this heavenly position according to Hebrews 12:1, 22-24?

a. (v.1)_____ e. (v.23) _____

b. (v.22) _____ f. (v.23) _____

c. (v.22) _____ g. (v.24) _____

d. (v.23) _____ h. (v.24)_____

4. Since this is our position, what then are we exhorted to do? (Col. 3:1-2)

a. _____

b. _____

5. Seated in heavenly places with Jesus, what are we looking for? (Phil. 3:20-21)

a. _____

b. _____

6. What are two things that we must follow after if we want to see the Lord? (Heb. 12:14)

a. _____

b. _____

7. What is the Hope that leads us to live a pure life? (I John 3:1-3)

_____

8. By what power will we be changed into His likeness? (Phil. 3:21)

_____

9. What will be the Christian's crown and joy in the day of the Lord? (Phil. 4:1; I Thes. 2:19-20)

_____

10. Paul exhorts the believers again to stand fast in the Lord. What does he mean by this? (Phil. 1:27)

a. _____

b. _____

c. _____

d. _____

STUDY 5

OUR CHRISTIAN RESPONSIBILITY

I. EXHORTATION TO UNITY, RESPONSIBILITY, AND PRAYER

1. What four things does Paul exhort the believers to do? (Phil. 4:2-5)
   a. (v.2) _____
   b. (v.3) _____
   c. (v.4) _____
   d. (v.5) _____

2. What are the believer's responsibilities to those who labor among them? (I Tim. 5:17-18; I Cor. 9:7-14)
   a. _____
   b. _____
   c. _____

3. What guidelines for prayer does Paul give? (Phil. 4:6)
   a. _____
   b. _____
   c. _____

4. What will be the result of praying in the above manner? (Phil. 4:7)
   _____
   _____

5. What promise does Paul base his knowledge of prayer on? (Ps. 55:22)
   Condition: _____
   Promise:
      1. _____
      2. _____

   (Prov. 16:3)
   Condition: _____
   _____
   Promise: _____

   (Ps. 37:5)
   Condition:
      1. _____
      2. _____
   Promise: _____

6. Paul tells us that praying in this manner will produce the peace of God in our lives. Is peace our legal right, and where was the provision for our peace made? (Is. 53:5)
   _____
   _____

We have recognized that the atonement has provided forgiveness of sins, healing, but we have overlooked the precious provision for peace. It is this peace that the world is looking for.

7. How can we remain in perfect peace? (Is. 26:3; Rom. 8:6)

    a. _____

    b. _____

If we begin to experience a lack of peace, it is evident that we have taken our eyes off Jesus and have quit trusting Him. Lack of peace is lack of trust.

8. In the last days, what will be the characteristic of the Church, the body of believers, who are the temple of the living God? (Hag. 2:9)

    a. _____

    b. _____

We see then that this quality of peace is the quality of a truly spiritual person. As we cast all our care upon Him, totally trusting in and relying on, and cleaving to God and His Word, this peace will well up within us and flow out to others.

II. EXHORTATION TO PURITY OF MIND, VICTORY OVER CIRCUMSTANCES, AND THE BLESSINGS OF GIVING

1. Paul exhorts us earlier in this epistle to have the same mind in us that was in Jesus. In order to have a spiritual mind and to accomplish this, what things does Paul tell us to fill our mind with? (Phil. 4:8)

    a. _____ e. _____

    b. _____ f. _____

    c. _____ g. _____

    d. _____ h. _____

2. In verse 10, Paul thanks the Philippans for their care of him and for their ministry to him in in material things. Paul rejoices in the Lord because of this blessing. However, what is Paul's attitude? (Phil. 4:11-13)

    a. (v.11) _____

    b. (v.12) _____

    c. (v.12) _____

    d. (v.12) _____

    e. (v.12) _____

    f. (v.13) _____

We see from Paul's attitude that his trials and tribulations have worked their perfect work in his life. Here Paul reflects the ability to live above any circumstances. The circumstances no longer control Paul. He is moved and controlled only by the Spirit and his rejoicing in the Lord.

3. In the following verses, Paul commends the Philippians for their offering to him. What three things does Paul say concerning the blessings they shall receive from giving? (Phil. 4:17-19)

    a. (v.17) _____

    _____

    b. (v.18) _____

    _____

    c. (v.19) _____

    _____

4. We see here the principle that Jesus taught. What is that principle? (Luke 6:38)

   _____

5. Paul closes this epistle from prison with a note of victory. He sends greetings to the believers from the fruit of his labor even while in prison. Who were these people? (Phil. 4:22)

   _____

—NOTES—

SUMMARY

1. We see in Paul an example set forth that we would do well to follow. In the midst of terrible circumstances, we see Paul reigning as victor. *Paul is filled with Christ.* He is filled with the desire to press on in God, to know the Savior more deeply, and to be a partaker with Him in all things, even to suffer for His sake.

2. Paul is *filled with joy and praise.* Prison walls could not restrain Paul's song of rejoicing in his ever-present Lord. Paul truly demonstrates through his attitude a life filled with praise to God under all circumstances. Prison walls and chains could not stop Paul's song and testimony. So great was his witness that even members of Caesar's household were converted to the Lord.

3. Paul demonstrates a life that is *full of holiness.* Paul's heart and mind were set upon one thing—the glory of his God and Savior. Paul longed to see this holiness of mind and heart, the very mind of Christ reproduced in his fellow believers.

4. Paul demonstrates a life that is *full of love and fellowship* toward his fellow-believers. Paul, though imprisoned, seeks not to be ministered to, but to minister. His concern and burden of heart is to see his brethren grow and progress in the Lord. Paul's life demonstrates the bonds of love which bind him with his fellow-believers. It is written in I John 3:16:
"Hereby perceive we the love of God because he laid down his life for us; we ought to lay down our lives for the brethren."

And in John 15:12-13 Jesus said:

"This is my commandment that ye love one another as I have loved you. Greater love has no man than this, that a man lay down his life for his friends."

Paul says in Phil. 2:17-18: (Living Bible)

"And if my lifeblood is, so to speak, to be poured out over your faith which I am offering up to God as a sacrifice—even then I will be glad, and will share my joy with each of you. For you should be happy about this, too, and rejoice with me for having this privilege of dying for you."

Paul's life was a demonstration of *true* love. His life was an example of the two great commandments that Jesus gave.

1. "Love the Lord thy God with all thy *heart,* with all thy *mind,* with all thy *soul*, with all thy *strength.*"

The second is like the first—

2. "Love thy neighbor as thyself."

Paul's life was a demonstration of commitment to God and to his brothers. His life was a demonstration of the nature of God, for God is *love.*

—NOTES—

ANSWERS

"Who is like the wise man and who
knows the interpretation of a matter?
A man's wisdom illumines him and
causes his stern face to beam."
Ecclesiastes 8:1

INTRODUCTION

Correct Answers

1. He who began a good work in you will perfect it until the day of Christ Jesus.
2. a. I thank my God in all my remembrance of you.
   b. Always offering prayer with joy for them.
   c. Thanks God for their participation in the gospel.
   d. I have you in my heart.
   e. They stood with him in the preaching of the gospel.
   f. I long for you with the affection of Christ Jesus.

STUDY 1

THE ALL-SUFFICIENCY
OF CHRIST

Correct Answers

I. CHRIST, THE CHRISTIAN'S LIFE: REJOICING IN SPITE OF SUFFERING

1. a. That your love may abound still more and more in real knowledge and all discernment.
   b. That you may approve the things that are excellent.
   c. That you may be sincere and blameless.
   d. That we will be filled with the fruit of righteousness.
2. a. Jesus.
   b. The Church.
3. a. The spirit of wisdom and understanding.
   b. The spirit of counsel and strength.
   c. The spirit of knowledge and the fear of the Lord.
4. a. He will delight in the fear of the Lord.
   b. He will not judge by what his eyes see.
   c. He will not make a decision by what his ears hear.
   d. With righteousness he will judge the poor.
   e. He will decide with fairness for the afflicted of the earth.
   f. He will stride the earth with the rod of his mouth.
   g. With the breath of his lips he will slay the wicked.
   h. Righteousness will be the belt about his loins.
   i. Faithfulness the belt about his waist.
5. He is rejoicing.
6. a. That his circumstances had turned out for the greater progress of the gospel.
   b. The cause of Christ had become known throughout the whole praetorian guard and to everyone else.
   c. Other brothers had more courage to speak the Word of God without fear.
   d. Christ was proclaimed.
7. a. That he should not be put to shame in anything.
   b. Christ shall be exalted in my body, by life or by death.
   c. To live is Christ, to die is gain.
8. To be with Christ.
   a. To be absent from the body is to be at home with the Lord.
9. It was more necessary to minister to the saints.
10. a. Standing firm.
    b. In one spirit.
    c. With one mind striving together for the faith of the gospel.
    d. In no way alarmed by your opponents.
11. a. To the enemies, a sign of destruction.
    b. To you, a sign of salvation, and that from God.
12. It is only just for God to repay those who afflict you.
13. Vengeance is Mine, I will repay.
14. Do not take vengeance, nor bear any grudge against the sons of your people but you are to love your neighbor as yourself.
15. That we may be considered worthy of the Kingdom of God and that God might count us worthy of our calling.
16. It is producing within us an eternal weight of glory.
17. We shall be glorified with Him.
18. The fiery ordeal.
19. a. It is for your testing.
    b. Keep on rejoicing.

20. The Spirit of glory and of God is resting upon you.
21. Let him glorify God.
22. At the household of God.
23. The salvation of the righteous.
24. a. A tree of life.
    b. He captures lives for God.
25. To that age and the resurrection of the dead.
26. The resurrection of the dead.
27. a. Run in such a way that you may win.
    b. Exercise self control in all things.
    c. Run with the goal in mind.
    d. Buffet your body and make it your slave.
28. That he might not be disqualified.
29. a. Sons of God.
    b. Sons of the Resurrection.
30. Holiness.
31. They did not yield or back down.
32. a. Entrust your soul to God.
    b. Do what is right.
33. To suffer for His sake.

II. CHRIST, THE CHRISTIAN'S PATTERN: REJOICING IN LOWLY SERVICE

1. a. Be of the same mind.
   b. Maintain the same love.
   c. United in spirit.
   d. Intent on one purpose.
   e. Do nothing from selfishness or empty conceit.
   f. With humility of mind let each of you regard one another as more important than himself.
   g. Do not merely look out for your own personal interests, but also for the interests of others.
2. The attitude of Christ.
3. a. Did not regard equality with God a thing to be grasped.
   b. Emptied Himself.
   c. Took on the form of a bondservant.
   d. Was made in the likeness of man.
   e. Humbled Himself.
   f. Became obedient to the point of death.
4. By the Holy Spirit.
5. No.
6. a. God highly exalted Him.
   b. Bestowed on Him the name which is above every name.
7. a. Younger men, be subject to your elders.
   b. All clothe yourselves with humility toward one another.
   c. Humble yourselves under the mighty hand of God.
8. He will exalt you at the proper time.
9. a. At that name every knee shall bow.
   b. Every tongue shall confess that Jesus Christ is Lord.
10. a. Those in heaven.
    b. Those on earth.
    c. Those under the earth.
11. To obtain salvation through our Lord Jesus Christ.
12. a. Spirit.
    b. Soul.
    c. Body.

13. a. He that has called you—Jesus.
    b. The Spirit.
14. By obedience to the truth.
15. a. Avoid worldly and empty chatter.
    b. Abstain from wickedness.
    c. Flee from youthful lusts.
    d. Pursue righteousness, faith, love, and peace with those who call on the Lord from a pure heart.
16. Be all the more diligent to make certain about His calling and choosing you.
17. a. Through the true knowledge of Him we have everything pertaining to life and godliness.
    b. By the promises you become partakers of the divine nature.
    c. Apply all diligence.
    d. In your faith supply moral excellence.
    e. In your moral excellence, knowledge.
    f. In your knowledge, self-control.
    g. In your self-control, perserverance.
    h. In your perserverance, godliness.
    i. In your godliness, brotherly kindness.
    j. In your brotherly kindness, Christian love.
18. The entrance into the eternal kingdom will be abundantly supplied to you.
19. It is God who is at work in you.
20. a. Blameless and innocent.
    b. Children of God.
    c. Above reproach.
    d. Appearing as lights in the midst of a crooked and perverse generation.
    e. Holding fast the word of life.
    f. In the day of Christ there will be cause to glory.
21. a. For Jesus.
    b. For the sake of the gospel.
22. Because David desired to do all God's will.
23. a. I can do nothing on my own.
    b. Because I do not seek my own will but the will of Him who sent me.
24. Torches.
25. The torches were seen, they blew the trumpets and cried out, "a sword for the Lord and for Gideon."

THE TRUE SERVANTS
OF GOD

Correct Answers

I. THE FELLOWSHIP AND LOVE OF THE SAINTS

1. I am being poured out as a drink offering.
2. That one lay down his life for his friends.
3. a. Love is as strong as death.
   b. Many waters cannot quench love.
   c. Nor will the rivers overflow it.
   d. If a man were to give all for love, it would be despised.
4. Being fitted and held together by that which every joint supplies, according to the proper working of each individual part, causes the growth of the body for the building up of itself in love.
5. We will be filled with the fulness of God.
6. Love.
7. a. Paul received encouragement, knowing of the welfare of the church.
   b. Timothy shared Pauls love and concern for the brethren.
   c. Paul took Timothy as his son.
   d. Epaphroditus was Paul's fellow-worker and fellow-soldier.
   e. Epaphroditus is also your messenger and minister to my need.
   f. The church at Philippi sent Epaphroditus to minister.
   g. Epaphroditus longed after the church at Philippi.
   h. He was distressed because they had heard he was sick.
   i. Paul was sorrowful because of Epaphroditus' illness.
   j. Paul was happy to know that the church would rejoice to see Epaphroditus.
   k. Because of the work of Christ, Epaphroditus came close to death.
8. He was overworked.

II. WARNING AGAINST FALSE PROPHETS AND TEACHERS

1. a. Beware of the dogs.
   b. Beware of the evil workers.
   c. Beware of the false circumcision.
2. a. The watchmen (pastors and shepherds) that are blind.
   b. They know nothing (ignorant of the Word).
   c. They are dumb dogs unable to bark (no warning of judgment).
   d. Dreamers lying down, who love to slumber.
   e. Greedy, not satisfied.
   f. Shepherds who have no understanding.
   g. They have all turned to their own way—seeking to build their own kingdom.
   h. They fill others with strong wine.
   i. They think that tomorrow will be like today, only more so.
3. The word of the Lord has become a reproach to them.
4. a. Every one is greedy for gain.
   b. Every one deals falsely.
   c. They have healed the wound of My people slightly.
   d. They say, ''peace, peace,'' when there is no peace.
   e. They were not ashamed of their abominations—no repentance.

f. They would not walk in the ways of the Lord.

g. They will not listen to God's prophets.

h. They would not listen to the Word, but rejected it.

5. a. Those who worship in the Spirit of God.

   b. Those who glory in Christ Jesus.

   c. Those who put no confidence in the flesh.

   d. He is a Jew who is one inwardly.

   e. Has been circumcised in heart.

   f. By the Spirit, not by the letter.

   g. His praise is not from men, but from God.

6. a. All who believe.

   b. Those who follow in the steps of the faith of Abraham.

7. a. If you belong to Christ, then you are Abraham's offspring.

   b. You are heirs according to the promise.

   c. In Christ Jesus, the blessing of Abraham comes to the Gentiles.

   d. We receive the promise of the Spirit through faith.

8. a. Circumcised the eighth day.

   b. Full-blooded Jew.

   c. Of the tribe of Benjamin.

   d. A Hebrew of Hebrews.

   e. Pharisee.

   f. His religious zeal was shown by his persecution of the Church.

   g. According to the law, found blameless.

9. a. What things were gain to him, he counted as loss.

   b. He counted all things to be loss in view of the surpassing value of knowing Christ.

   c. Counted his works as rubbish in order that he might gain Christ.

10. Put no confidence in the flesh.

11. a. Be found in Him.

   b. Not having a righteousness of his own.

   c. Having the righteousness which comes by faith.

12. No man should boast before God.

13. The Lord Jesus Christ.

14. That we understand and know God.

THE HIGH
CALLING OF GOD

Correct Answers

I. THE CRY OF PAUL'S HEART

1. a. That I may know Him.
   b. That I may know the power of His resurrection.
   c. The fellowship of His sufferings.
   d. Being conformed to His death.
2. That they may know Thee, the only true God, and Jesus Christ.
3. a. May he kiss me with the kisses of his mouth.
   b. Your love is better than wine.
   c. Your name is like purified oil.
   d. Draw me after you and let us run together.
   e. The king has brought me into his chamber.
   f. We will rejoice in you and be glad.
   g. We will extol your love more than wine.
   h. Rightly do they love you.
4. a. I led them with cords of a man, with bonds of love.
   b. I became to them as one who lifts the yoke from their jaws.
   c. I bent down and fed them.
5. a. That he might be glorified with Him.
   b. If we endure, we shall reign with Him.
   c. The Spirit of glory and of God rests upon you.
6. a. That the life of Jesus may be manifested in our body.
   b. If we die with Him, we shall also live with Him.
   c. We will walk in newness of life.
   d. We shall be in the likeness of His resurrection.
   e. If you die you will bring forth much fruit.
7. a. To obtain salvation through our Lord Jesus Christ.
   b. To gain the glory of our Lord Jesus Christ.
8. a. Spirit.
   b. Soul.
   c. Body.
9. The Lord.

II. REDEMPTION OF THE SOUL

1. a. As we, with unveiled face, behold as in a mirror the glory of the Lord (by looking into the Word), we are transformed into the same image by the Spirit.
   b. In humility receive the word implanted, which is able to save your souls.
2. Being a doer of the Word and not a hearer only.
3. a. All glorious within.
   b. Clothing is interwoven with gold (the nature of God).
   c. Will be led to the King in embroidered work.
4. a. My dove (completely led by the Spirit).
   b. My perfect one.
   c. Unique.
   d. She is the pure child of the one who bore her.

        e. Grows like the dawn.
        f. As beautiful as the moon.
        g. As pure as the sun.
        h. As awesome as an army with banners.
    5. To become conformed to the image of His Son.
    6. The salvation of your soul.

III. REDEMPTION OF THE BODY

    1. He will give life to your mortal bodies through His Spirit who indwells you.
    2. a. He heals all your diseases.
        b. He redeems your life from the pit.
        c. Your youth is renewed like the eagle.
        d. He gives strength to the weary.
        e. To him who lacks might, He increases power.
        f. Those who wait for the Lord will gain new strength.
        g. They will run and not get tired.
        h. They will walk and not become weary.
    3. a. Joshua was as strong at 85 as he was at 40.
        b. Enoch lived 365 years and never died. Methuselah lived 969 years.
        c. Elijah was taken to heaven and did not have to die.
    4. a. To be clothed with our dwelling from heaven (immortality).
        b. Groaning not to be found naked.
        c. Not to be unclothed (death).
        d. That that which is mortal may be swallowed up by life.
    5. God prepared us for this very purpose.
    6. Put all things in subjection under our feet.
    7. Now we do not yet see all things subjected to us.
    8. a. Tasted death for every man.
        b. He rendered powerless him who had the power of death, the devil.
        c. He delivered us from the fear of death.
    9. a. Abolished death.
        b. Brought life and immortality to light through the gospel.
    10. The law of sin and of death.
    11. It wasn't God's time.
    12. Yes.
    13. No.
    14. a. There is an appointed time.
        b. A people yet to be created will praise the Lord.
    15. The time will come when the saints take possession of the kingdom.
    16. a. The saints of the Highest One will receive the kingdom.
        b. They will possess the kingdom forever.
        c. The court will sit for judgment.
        d. His (Satan's) dominion will be taken away, annihilated and destroyed forever.
        e. The sovereignty, the dominion and the greatness of all the kingdoms will be given to the saints.
    17. a. The Lord will shake the heavens and the earth.
        b. He will overthrow the thrones of kingdoms and destroy the power of the kingdoms of the nations.
        c. He will make you like a signet ring.
    18. a. You will have the Lord for an everlasting light.
        b. Your sun will set no more.
        c. All your people will be righteous.
        d. They will possess the land forever.

e. That He may be glorified.

f. The smallest one will become a clan, and the least one a mighty nation.

19. The Lord will hasten it in its time.

20. Every pot in Jerusalem and in Judah will be holy to the Lord of Hosts.

21. a. They will be mine.

b. I will spare them.

c. You will distinguish between the righteous and the wicked.

d. The wicked will be burnt.

e. The sun of righteousness will rise with healing in its wings.

f. You will go forth and skip about like calves from the stall.

g. You will tread down the wicked.

22. a. The revealing of the sons of God.

b. To be set free from its slavery to corruption into the freedom of the glory of the children of God.

c. Adoption as sons, the redemption of our body.

23. In the last time.

24. a. When He has abolished all rule and all authority and power.

b. Until He has put all His enemies under His feet.

25. Death.

26. a. Forget what lies behind.

b. Reach forward to what lies ahead.

c. Press on toward the goal for the prize of the upward call of God in Christ Jesus.

d. As many as are perfect, having this attitude.

STUDY 4

EXHORTATION TO
HOLYMINDEDNESS

Correct Answers

I. EXHORTATION TO WALK IN THE TRUTH YOU HAVE RECEIVED

1. Let us keep living by that same standard to which we have attained.
2. a. We must pay much closer attention to what we have heard, lest we drift away from it.
   b. How shall we escape if we neglect so great a salvation?
3. a. What you have, hold fast until I come.
   b. He who overcomes, and he who keeps My deeds until the end, to him I will give authority over the nations.
4. a. Holy conduct and godliness.
   b. Looking for and hastening the coming of the day of God.
   c. Be diligent to be found by Him in peace.
   d. Be found spotless.
   e. Be found blameless.
   f. Be on your guard against error, lest you fall.

II. EXHORTATION TO WALK IN THE EXAMPLE OF THE GODLY

1. a. Join in following my example.
   b. Observe those who walk according to the pattern you have in us.
2. a. The things you have learned from me.
   b. The things you have received from me.
   c. The things you have heard from me.
   d. The things you have seen in me.
3. a. In speech.
   b. Conduct.
   c. Love.
   d. Faith.
   e. Purity.
   f. Give attention to the public reading of Scripture.
   g. Give attention to exhortation.
   h. Give attention to teaching.
   i. Do not neglect the spiritual gift within you.
4. Aged Men
   a. Temperate.
   b. Dignified.
   c. Sensible.
   d. Sound in faith.
   e. Sound in love.
   f. Sound in perserverance.

Aged Women and Young Women
a. Reverent in behavior.
b. Not malicious gossips.
c. Not enslaved to much wine.
d. Teaching what is good.
e. Love their husbands.
f. Love their children.
g. Sensible.
h. Pure.
i. Workers at home.
j. Kind.
k. Subject to their own husbands.
Young Men
a. Sensible.
b. Example of good deeds.
c. Purity in doctrine.
d. Dignified.
e. Sound in speech.
Servants
a. Be subject to your own masters in everything.
b. Be well-pleasing.
c. Not argumentative.
d. Not pilfering.
e. Showing all good faith.

III. EXHORTATION TO BEWARE OF ENEMIES OF THE CROSS

1. Enemies of the cross of Christ.
2. a. Their end is destruction.
   b. Whose god is their appetite.
   c. Whose glory is in their shame.
   d. Set their minds on earthly things.
3. a. Indulge the flesh in its corrupt desires.
   b. Despise authority.
   c. Daring.
   d. Self-willed.
   e. Do not tremble when they revile angelic majesties.
4. a. He is conceited.
   b. Understands nothing.
   c. Has a morbid interest in controversial questions, disputes about words.
   d. Deprived of the truth.
   e. Suppose that godliness is a means of gain.
5. a. Envy.
   b. Strife.
   c. Abusive language.
   d. Evil suspicions.
   e. Constant friction.
6. a. Keep your eye on them.
   b. Turn away from them.
7. a. By smooth speech.
   b. By flattering speech.

IV. EXHORTATION TO SET OUR MIND ON HEAVENLY THINGS

1. In heaven.
2. In the heavenly places in Christ Jesus.
3. a. We have so great a cloud of witnesses surrounding us.
   b. Mount Zion, the heavenly Jerusalem.
   c. Myriads of angels.
   d. The general assembly and church of the first-born.
   e. God, the judge of all.
   f. The spirits of righteous men made perfect.
   g. Jesus, the mediator.
   h. The sprinkled blood.
4. a. Keep seeking the things above.
   b. Set your mind on the things above.
5. a. A Savior, the Lord Jesus Christ.
   b. Redemption of our body.
6. a. Peace with all men.
   b. Sanctification.
7. When He appears, we shall be like Him.
8. By His power.
9. Those that he has won to Christ and discipled.
10. a. Conduct yourself in a manner worthy of the gospel.
    b. Stand firm in one spirit.
    c. With one mind.
    d. Strive together for the faith of the gospel.

STUDY 5

OUR CHRISTIAN RESPONSIBILITY

Correct Answers

I. EXHORTATION TO UNITY, RESPONSIBILITY AND TO PRAYER

1. a. Live in harmony in the Lord.
   b. Help those who have labored in the gospel.
   c. Rejoice in the Lord always.
   d. Let your forbearing spirit be known to all men.
2. a. Let the elders be considered worthy of double honor.
   b. The laborer is worthy of his wages.
   c. Those who proclaim the gospel are to get their living from the gospel.
3. a. Be anxious for nothing.
   b. Pray and supplicate in everything.
   c. With thanksgiving.
4. The peace of God, which surpasses all comprehension, shall guard your hearts and your minds.
   Contition: Cast your burden upon the Lord.
   Promise: 1) He will sustain you.
              2) He will never allow the righteous to be shaken.
   Condition: Commit your works to the Lord.
   Promise: Your plans will be established.
   Condition: 1) Commit your way to the Lord.
               2) Trust also in Him.
   Promise: He will do it.
6. Yes, the provision for our peace was made in the atonement. The chastening for our well-being (peace) fell upon Him.
7. a. Keep our mind steadfast on the Lord and trust in Him.
   b. Set our mind on the Spirit.
8. a. The latter glory of this house will be greater than the former.
   b. In this place I shall give peace.

II. EXHORTATION TO PURITY OF MIND, VICTORY OVER CIRCUMSTANCES, AND THE BLESSINGS OF GIVING

1. a. True.
   b. Honorable.
   c. Right.
   d. Pure.
   e. Lovely.
   f. Of good repute.
   g. Any excellence.
   h. Anything worthy of praise.
2. a. Learned to be content in whatever circumstance I am in.
   b. Know how to get along with humble means.
   c. Know how to live in prosperity.
   d. Learned the secret of being filled and going hungry.
   e. Learned the secret of having abundance and suffering need.
   f. I can do all things through Him who strengthens me.
3. a. He was seeking for the profit which increases to their account.
   b. What they sent was an acceptable sacrifice, well-pleasing to God.
   c. My God shall supply all your needs according to His riches in glory in Christ Jesus.
4. Give, and it will be given to you.
5. Those of Caesar's household.

Life Changing Historical Reprints

from Maranatha Publications

The Story of Liberty

originally published in 1879.

The secular humanists have edited God out of history! Now you can read what they cut out. Reprinted from the original 1879 edition, *The Story of Liberty* tells you the price that was paid for our freedom and how it was won. An excellent historical resource for your library. This is our best seller among home schools and Christian educators. Paperback, illustrated, 415 pages, $14.95 ISBN 0-938558-20-X

The Story of Liberty Study Guide – Written by Steve Dawson, this workbook offers 98 pages of challenging comprehensive questions that allow the reader to fill-in-the-blank as they progress through this valuable study book. $10.95 ISBN 0-938558-27-7

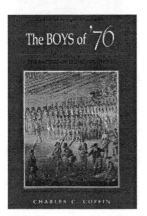

Sweet Land of Liberty

originally published in 1881 and titled *Old Times in the Colonies*

Sweet Land of Liberty is the sequel to *The Story of Liberty*. It tells the historical highlights of colonial America from a Providential view. This volume covers the period from the discovery and settlement of America to the Revolutionary War. Written by Civil War correspondent and children's author Charles Coffin, *Sweet Land of Liberty* has been faithfully reproduced exactly as it was originally printed in 1881. Paperback, illustrated, 458 pages, $14.95 ISBN 0-938558-48-X

The Boys of '76

reprinted from the original 1876 manuscript

In this powerful volume an attempt has been made to give a concise, plain, and authentic narrative of the principal battles of the Revolution as witnessed by those who took part in them. More than a century has passed since "*The Boys of '76*" shouldered their muskets and fought for their liberties. Author Charles Coffin brings to life the battles of the Revolution from "The Alarm" proclaimed in Concord in 1775, to the surrender of the British army in 1981. Paperback, illustrated, 423 pages, $16.95. ISBN 0-938558-82-X

"An accurate story of our nation's fight for liberty. I pray everyone, young and old alike, will read and remember *The Boys of '76*."

Greg Harris, Director of Noble Institute and author of *The Christian Home School*

Life Changing Books
& Bible Studies
from Maranatha Publications

Bible Study Series

Firm
Foundation

This study is our best seller. Covers the foundational truths in Scripture. Includes repentance, baptism, healing, faith, and other studies. Paperback, 125 pages, $9.95
ISBN # 0-938553-005

Overcoming
Life

Takes you a step further than the basics. Includes a series on brokenness, as well as faith, righteousness, and the work of the ministry. Paperback, 113 pages, $9.95
ISBN # 0-938558-01-3

Lovers
of God

Life Changing truths from Philippians. The all-sufficiency of God, living in joy, victory over trials, having the mind of Christ, and fruitfulness in ministry. Paperback, 43 pages, $7.95
ISBN # 0-938558-03-X

Preparation
of the Bride

Explains metaphors and hidden truths in the Song of Solomon. This study reveals the beauty of the union between Jesus and His Bride. Paperback, 234 pages, $14.95
ISBN # 0-88270-471-0

Life of
Excellence

Help for building character in your Christian life... bridling the tongue, godly wisdom, our attitude toward sinners, living in the last days, and more. Paperback, 60 pages, $7.95
ISBN # 0-938558-04-8

Estudios Biblicos para un Fundamento Firmé

Firm Foundation Also Available in Spanish!

An interactive Bible Study that challenges the reader to utilize their Bible and seek out truths in Scripture. This top selling Bible study is used around the world. Paperback, 125 pages, $9.95
ISBN # 0-938558-22-6

MARANATHA PUBLICATIONS, INC.

P. O. BOX 1799 • GAINESVILLE, FL 32602 • 352-375-6000 • FAX 352-335-0080

Bible Study Books — *by Bob and Rose Weiner*

BOOK NAME	PRICE	QUANTITY	TOTAL
Firm Foundation	$ 9.95		
Overcoming Life	$ 9.95		
Lovers of God	$ 7.95		
Life of Excellence	$ 7.95		
Preparation of the Bride	$14.95		
One Set of Above Studies (5)	$49.95		
Jesus Brings New Life	$ 3.95		
Spanish Firm Foundation	$ 9.95		

Christian History Books

BOOK NAME	PRICE	QUANTITY	TOTAL
The Story of Liberty (A Christian History Text)	$14.95		
Story of Liberty Study Guide - by Steve Dawson	$ 10.95		
Sweet Land of Liberty (Sequel to Story of Liberty)	$14.95		
The Boys of '76 (Sequel to Sweet Land of Liberty)	$16.95		

Booklets

BOOK NAME	PRICE	QUANTITY	TOTAL
— by Bob and Rose Weiner			
How to Become a Dynamic Speaker	$ 2.50		
Mightier Than The Sword	$ 2.50		
The Bed Is Too Short	$ 2.50		
Christian Dominion	$ 2.50		
— by Lee Grady			
Defending Christian Economics	$ 2.50		
A Vision For World Dominion	$ 2.50		
War of the Words	$ 2.50		

Sub Total	
Shipping	
Add FL sales tax	
TOTAL US Dollars	

VISA and MasterCard Accepted

Ship To:

Name _____

Address _____

City _____

State _____ Zip _____

Phone (_____) _____

❑ Check enclosed, payable to Maranatha Publications, Inc.

❑ Charge to my: ❑ VISA ❑ MasterCard

Card No. _____ Expires ____/____

Shipping & Handling:

Less than $10.00	$3.50
$10.00 - $24.99	$4.50
$25.00 - $49.99	$5.50
$50.00 or more	9%

Mail Order To: **Maranatha Publications, Inc., P.O. Box 1799, Gainesville, FL 32602**